WANTED:

MYSTERY INVESTIGATORS

Are you looking for adventure? Are you curious? Do you like solving challenges — and, most of all, do you want to dig into some of the most deeply-buried Great Mysteries of the World?

YOU

Adventurous?

Like a challenge?

Curious?

RICHARD

Adventurous? (Adventure is fine as long as there are no big spiders . . . eek!)

Like a challenge? (There's nothing I like better than really challenging challenges!)

Curious? (Oh yes! Some might say 'nosy'.)

If you can tick all the boxes, join me on a global journey to investigate the unexplained, the bizarre and the downright weird. From cursed pharaohs and pirate caves, to imaginary kingdoms and magical skulls, you'll be stunned at some of the strange and sp[ ]goings-on aroun[ ]

All these mysteries have baffled the experts and left investigators clueless. My mission is to find out the truth. And I need your help.

Together, we'll weigh up the evidence, look at all the explanations — then you decide which is the best solution. You can even keep track of your solved mysteries by turning to page 105 and recording your verdict!

A word of warning: If you're the nervous type, put this book down now. Some of the mysteries we'll be investigating are pretty scary. The kind of things that might make a person a bit, well, jumpy . . .

What was that?

Did you hear something?

OK, I'd better calm down . . . and breathe . . .

Let's go. Time to explore the world's greatest mysteries!

Richard Hammond

RICHARD HAMMOND'S

GREAT MYSTERIES OF THE WORLD

ANCIENT TREASURES

RED FOX

RICHARD HAMMOND'S GREAT MYSTERIES OF THE WORLD: ANCIENT TREASURES
A RED FOX BOOK 978 1 849 41715 0

Published in Great Britain by Red Fox,
an imprint of Random House Children's Publishers UK
A Random House Group Company
1 3 5 7 9 10 8 6 4 2

Bind-up edition published by The Bodley Head 2013
This Red Fox edition published 2014

The Random House Group Limited supports the Forest Stewardship Council® (FSC®),
the leading international forest-certification organisation. Our books carrying the FSC label
are printed on FSC®-certified paper. FSC is the only forest-certification scheme supported
by the leading environmental organisations, including Greenpeace. Our paper procurement
policy can be found at www.randomhouse.co.uk/environment

Set in Baskerville Classico 12/17.5pt

RANDOM HOUSE CHILDREN'S PUBLISHERS UK
61–63 Uxbridge Road, London W5 5SA

www.**randomhousechildrens**.co.uk
www.**totallyrandombooks**.co.uk
www.**randomhouse**.co.uk

Addresses for companies within The Random House Group Limited can be found at:
www.randomhouse.co.uk/offices.htm

THE RANDOM HOUSE GROUP Limited Reg. No. 954009

A CIP catalogue record for this book is available from the British Library.

Printed and bound in Great Britain by
CPI Group (UK) Ltd, Croydon, CR0 4YY

With special thanks to Amanda Li

CONTENTS

MYSTERY
1

Pirate Treasure

THE MISSION ...

... to find out if there are hoards of pirate treasure out there,
just waiting to be found ...

BURNING QUESTIONS
🔥 Did pirates really bury their treasure?
🔥 Did they make maps to find it again?
🔥 Where did the treasure come from?

*Hoards of glittering
treasure – 'chest'
what a pirate needs!*

MISSION DETAILS

Ahhaaar, me hearties! Yo ho ho and a bottle of rum! Heave ho! Land ahoy! Shiver me timbers!

Talking like a pirate – brilliant! *Ahhaarrr!!* I could do it all day. Actually, I tried to once, but Mrs Hamster got a bit tired of it and made me stop.

Pirates are just the best though, aren't they? I mean, they had the best outfits for a start – it's the only thing I'll wear to a fancy-dress party, whatever the theme. And they did all the best stuff.

- They went on thrilling voyages across the seven seas
- They flew skull-and-crossbone flags and fought with swashbuckling swords . . .
- Some had talking parrots, hooks for hands and peg legs all at the same time! I should imagine a one-legged talking parrot that perched on a hook would have been worth a fortune.

Long John Silver, Captain Hook and Captain Jack Sparrow are just a few of the splendid sea dogs who have appeared in movies, TV shows and books. But what about *real* pirates? Was it all 'ha ha' and 'ho ho' on the high seas? Well, no, not quite.

In the past, being a pirate was a serious – and often deadly – business. All that sword-fighting and ship-burning and sailing to far-off places with unknown diseases was pretty

Eye-patch, parrot, earrings, hat – he's got all the pirate paraphernalia!

risky stuff. Plus, if you got caught by the authorities, you'd be hanged and your body left to rot in public. Not much of a welcome home after a long voyage . . .

Because it was so dangerous, some historians think that pirates of the past could have expected to live just two years. Two years? Perhaps a pirate's life wouldn't have been for me, after all . . .

So why did pirates risk their lives? For treasure, of course! (With a few bottles of rum thrown in.)

So jump on board to find out the truth about real pirates, and whether any of those famed pirate treasure chests are still out there . . .

THE LOCATION

Wherever there was a shipping route, there was probably a pirate. Ever since the first boats and ships set sail, pirates have been around to prey on them.

- 🌐 The ancient Greeks and the Romans were attacked by pirates in the Mediterranean Sea – the Roman emperor, Julius Caesar, was even kidnapped by them
- 🌐 Scandinavian Vikings were the bearded pirates of the north, raiding and invading in their longships
- 🌐 Chinese pirates in ships called junks ruled the seas around China up until the eighteenth century
- 🌐 And in the sixteenth century, pirates called corsairs sailed the Barbary Coast of North Africa

One of the most famous periods of pirate history was during the seventeenth and eighteenth centuries, when terrifying pirates like Blackbeard became legendary. They even called it the Golden Age of Piracy. I mean, probably not at the time, but we've certainly called it that since.

The Spanish had colonized the New World in the sixteenth century, taking huge territories in Central and South America. (See page 60 for more on the Spanish explorers.) Spanish ships called galleons carried fabulous wealth from these lands through the Caribbean and across the Atlantic back to Spain. And where there's a ship full of valuables, well yes, you guessed it, there's a pirate. The galleons, inevitably, were attacked by pirates, some of whom were called buccaneers – the real Pirates of the Caribbean ...

The Spanish Main – where pirates roamed the waters.

THE EVIDENCE

Pirates have been romanticized throughout history, but in reality, attacking and robbing ships at sea was nothing to be proud of. Pirates used threats and violence to steal pretty much anything they could. Silver, gold and other treasures were obviously at the top of a pirate's wish list, but food, drink and clothes were all taken on board, so to speak.

Pirate ships were usually smaller and speedier than the ones they preyed on. The pirates could sneak up alongside their chosen ship and leap aboard quickly, before the crew had a chance to defend themselves.

But, like everyone else, pirates had to stop and rest sometimes. And after months at sea (all that deck-swabbing, mainbrace-splicing and sea-shanty singing can be very tiring, you know) a pirate crew would need to find somewhere to land, stock up on food and drink, and perhaps do a spot of trading. Maybe even have a bit of entertainment?

Pirates were always on the lookout for 'pirate-friendly' places – and what better spot than a nice quiet island?

A desert island – every pirate's dream . . .

Let's find out more about a few pirates who used islands as hiding places . . .

The Life – and Death – of William Kidd

Legendary pirate William Kidd had a fearsome reputation. He once killed a member of his own crew by throwing a heavy iron bucket at him. That's one way to kick the bucket . . .

Kidd started off his pirating career as a privateer (I'll explain what one of those is in a minute), sailing to places like the West Indies and the Caribbean. He had plenty of

Here's looking at you, Kidd

piratical adventures, but his biggest haul was when he got his hands on a massive Armenian ship called the *Quedagh Merchant* in 1698. It was stuffed full of valuable silks, gold, silver and other riches. What a steal!

But this treasure trove was to be Kidd's downfall . . .

Two years before, Kidd had set sail on the *Adventure Galley*, with a crew of 80. His mission: to capture all French ships, plus any pirates in and around Madagascar. During the voyage the *Quedagh Merchant* was spotted in the distance, and Kidd did what any self-respecting pirate/privateer would do. He abandoned his own ship and took command of the much nicer new vessel.

But Kidd didn't know that some of the riches aboard the ship were owned by a powerful minister in India. The minister complained about Kidd, and the British government declared him a wanted criminal and known pirate. By this time Kidd was on his way to New York. When he arrived there, he was none too pleased to find himself arrested, then shipped back to England.

William Kidd was put on trial in 1701 and found – 'Guilty, m'lord.'

He was hanged at Execution Dock in London. Unfortunately, the first rope snapped and Kidd fell into the dirt below. No wonder his name was mud . . .

Another rope was found, and the second attempt was successful. Kidd's body was then covered in tar and suspended in chains as a warning to others. That's one way of 'hanging' around!

What happened to the treasure?

Before he reached New York with his loot, Kidd had heard the bad news of his forthcoming arrest. So he stopped at an island close to the coast – Gardiner's Island – to bury his treasure for safekeeping. He was hoping he'd be let off the charges and would soon be back.

Keep digging, men! Captain Kidd's in a 'hole' lot of trouble.

Kidd gave Mrs Gardiner (who owned Gardiner's Island) a length of gold cloth and a sack of sugar in return for letting him use her land. When he left, he warned the Gardiner family that if the treasure wasn't there when he got back, they'd be in big trouble . . . but of course, he never did make it back.

When Kidd was on trial, the Gardiners were ordered to produce his treasure as evidence. It was a stunning stash, containing:

 Bars of gold and silver

 Gold dust

 Glittering rubies, diamonds and other jewels

Rolls of luxurious silk

 57 bags of sugar (sugar was very valuable in those days: if you had a sweet tooth, you'd have needed a very big wallet, as well as a good dentist)

In November 1704 the treasure was sold off for a total of £6,437 (a lot of money in those days) and the cash was used to build a hospital. A plaque on Gardiner's Island marks the spot where the treasure was buried.

So – the treasure was found. But was it? Many believe that there is even more treasure that Kidd buried or hid during his adventures. Several locations have been suggested, mainly islands in Nova Scotia (a province of Canada) and Connecticut, USA. Others think that he might have buried his loot on a Caribbean island. Stories and rumours about the treasure are rife. Here's just one of them:

Dead Man's Creek ...

The story goes that Captain Kidd and his men went upriver searching for a place to bury their treasure. They found a good spot close to Clarke's Island, in the Connecticut river, Northfield, Massachusetts. Kidd then decided that something was needed to warn others away from the loot. Something really scary. What about a dead body? But whose ... ?

The men drew lots to see which of them would be the unlucky victim. The unfortunate pirate was 'despatched' and his body left to rot at the burial place.

Over the years a legend of a curse grew up around the treasure. It said that, if the gold was found, it could only be dug up if

three people did the digging at the same time (we have no idea why). They had to do it at midnight, and the full moon had to be directly overhead. The three diggers must form a triangle around the spot and work in silence. If anyone spoke, the mission would fail.

Unsurprisingly, the remainder of Kidd's treasure has never been found!

Pirate or Privateer?

What's the difference? They all did the same thing – attacking ships at sea.

A privateer, however, was a kind of 'official pirate' who had permission from his country to loot and plunder other ships. Privateers like William Kidd were sent by their governments to go on voyages and commandeer (which is just a nicer way of saying 'steal') enemy ships, also 'commandeering' their riches whilst they were at it. Of course, there was an official motive here: by taking over their enemy's ships, they weakened enemy naval forces, which came in very handy during a war. Any booty that the privateer found would be split between him, his crew and his government. Share and share alike!

Pirates, however, had no such permission and were working for themselves, as sort of self-employed villains. Unlike privateers, if they were caught, they could be hanged. Much riskier . . . but at least they were their own bosses.

> Captain Henry Morgan was a very famous privateer who worked for the English and fought the Spanish during the seventeenth century. He attacked cities as well as ships, and became extremely rich. He was eventually knighted by King Charles II and made governor of Jamaica. He even has a brand of rum named after him! Yo ho ho and a bottle of Captain Morgan!

William Kidd became a legendary figure in the years following his death – but are the stories of his missing buried treasure really true?

Here are some other famous pirates who were also said to have buried treasure . . .

Benito 'Bloody Sword' Bonito

BBSB, as we shall call him (though I shouldn't to his face, if you were to meet him) was a Portuguese pirate whose favourite activity was attacking and looting Spanish ships in the seas off Central America, then setting them on fire. He wasn't also nicknamed the 'Terror of the Atlantic' for nothing.

You can see where Benito got his nickname from. Check out the sword . . .

In 1819 Benito pulled off a famously cheeky stunt. He discovered that a huge amount of Spanish gold was being carried by mule overland to Acapulco, Mexico. So he and his men captured all the guards and dressed up in their uniforms. They coolly loaded the treasure straight onto Benito's own ship, the *Mary Deare*, then sailed to Cocos Island in the Pacific Ocean.

Benito was later killed, but his treasure was never found. Some think that his gold may be worth millions. And people are still looking for it . . .

What happened to the treasure?

The beautiful Cocos Island lies about 600 kilometres off the coast of Costa Rica. It has lush rainforests, roaring waterfalls, underground caves, even an ancient volcano. A fantastic place for a game of pirate hide-and-seek – and, of course, perfect for burying treasure . . .

A 1622 Spanish map showing the location of Cocos Island.

Cocos Island was once said to be a popular pirate hangout. The pirates would land there, find a good spot to bury their treasure – and hopefully remember where it was when they came back.

But, as you know, pirates didn't usually live very long (remember the two-year lifespan?). Many think that the island is still home to hoards of treasure, left by those unlucky pirates who perished elsewhere.

BBSB was one of them. He was said to have buried his treasure here under the cliffs – some say in a secret tunnel. It may still be there . . .

Captain Thompson and the Treasure of Lima

Cocos Island is thought to be the hiding place for another famous hoard of treasure, said to be worth hundreds of millions of pounds. It was brought here by an English captain, who disappeared, never to be seen again . . .

Hopeful treasure hunters should be on the lookout for:

 Two solid gold life-size statues of the Virgin Mary

273 jewelled swords

Candlesticks of gold and silver

Bars of solid gold

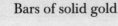

Hundreds of coins, diamonds and rubies

 Golden crowns . . . and more

Obviously if you're looking at that lot, then you've already found it and I suggest you nip to the bank. But where did it all come from?

The Treasure of Lima came from – no prizes for guessing – Lima, the capital city of Peru. In 1820 the Spanish ruled the region and were worried about a possible uprising against them. The governor of Lima asked a British trader called Captain Thompson to safeguard the valuable hoard (much of which came from local cathedrals and churches) on his vessel. The plan was eventually to ship it over to Mexico, where the Spanish also ruled.

But Captain Thompson betrayed the governor. He sailed straight for Cocos Island, where he and his crew buried the loot.

His plan was foiled when he and the crew were later captured by a Spanish warship. Most of the men were executed. Captain Thompson and his second-in command escaped death by promising to take the Spaniards to the treasure. They kept their word, but once they had all landed at Cocos Island, the pair quickly ran off into the forest.

Neither the men nor the treasure were ever found.

What happened to the treasure?

Over the years, many treasure hunters have landed on Cocos Island in the hope of getting rich. Even one of the presidents of the USA, Franklin Roosevelt, visited three times, hoping to strike gold.

One man was so sure that there was treasure on the island that he spent nearly 20 years searching for it. August Gissler, a German, arrived in 1889 – and didn't leave until 1908. In fact, he stayed for so long that the Costa Rican government made him the island's governor! But Gissler only ever found a few coins.

Why is the treasure so difficult to find? One of the problems is that the island has many networks of unexplored caves and tunnels – brilliant for hiding stuff, but not so great for finding it again. Over the years various earthquakes may have destroyed landmarks and features that would have helped identify its location.

In case you're wondering whether it's worth buying a plane ticket to Cocos Island for your summer holiday (and packing a metal detector), bear in mind that whoever finds the treasure probably won't be getting rich overnight. It would now automatically become the property of the Costa Rican government.

But fear not, my salty sea dogs! Cocos Island isn't the only island that is still rumoured to have treasure buried on it.

The Real Robinson Crusoe

Have you ever heard of *Robinson Crusoe*? It's a famous book written by Daniel Defoe, about an Englishman called Robinson Crusoe who is shipwrecked in 1659.

In the book, Crusoe is stranded on an island off the coast of Trinidad for a mammoth 28 years, two months and nineteen days. Crusoe knows this because he makes a notch with his knife in a piece of wood for every day that passes by (it must have been a very long piece of wood ...).

Crusoe – the most famous castaway in the world.

The desert island isn't the paradise of most castaways' dreams. Crusoe describes it as *'a dismal unfortunate island, which I call'd the Island of Despair.'*

Though, after 28 years, I'm not surprised he was a bit fed up with his surroundings!

During his very long stay, Robinson Crusoe survives a serious illness, an earthquake and violent hurricanes. And he later discovers that he is not alone –

Crusoe relieves the boredom by investigating a cave.

there are cannibals living on the island! When he rescues a man from the hungry cannibals' clutches, the man becomes Crusoe's friend. Crusoe calls him Friday, because he rescued him on a Friday. Simple, but easy to remember and better than calling him, say, 'Beans' because that's what he happened to have had for lunch that day. Or 'Headache' because he had one when he found him . . . you get my drift. Anyway, I digress . . .

Years later, when a shipload of mutineers turns up one day, Crusoe engineers an adventurous escape plan and returns by ship back to his life in England.

Now, Robinson Crusoe was a completely fictional character – but Daniel Defoe based his story on a real-life person: a privateer called Alexander Selkirk, who survived alone for four years after being left on an uninhabited island in the Pacific Ocean.

In 1704 Selkirk was on a privateering voyage as a member of the crew of the *Cinque Ports*. Following several violent clashes with the Spanish Armada, they stopped off at Más a Tierra (it wasn't called Robinson Crusoe Island then – because the book *Robinson Crusoe* hadn't yet been written, silly!). The crew were tired, hungry and sick, and the ship was badly damaged. Selkirk didn't think it would make the rest of the voyage and he argued with the captain about its seaworthiness. Whether Selkirk was deliberately marooned, or whether he thought it was safer to stay on the island rather than board the leaky old boat, we'll never know. But Selkirk never got back on the ship. Which was just as well, as it later sank, and most of the crew were drowned. A lucky escape . . .

For the next four years, Selkirk survived on fish, berries and wild goat (there were herds of them living on the island – in fact, they were his only company, apart from some rats and cats). Then, one day in 1709, he caught sight of a British ship passing by. Selkirk was picked up by a couple of privateers, and sailed back to London, where he became a mini-celebrity. Daniel Defoe heard his incredible story and *Robinson Crusoe* was published in 1719.

Now, Alexander Selkirk didn't have any treasure with him in 1704. So why is Robinson Crusoe Island – now famous for its castaway connection – also a top spot for treasure hunters?

Alexander Selkirk has fun playing with the local 'kids'.

The Real "Treasure Island"?

Like Cocos Island, Robinson Crusoe Island was a handy stop-off point for pirates. It is part of the archipelago of Juan Fernández in the Pacific Ocean, about 600 kilometres from the coast of Chile – but, more importantly, it was on one of the Spanish navigation routes. *Aharrr!*

Legend says that a Spanish galleon carrying treasures from South and Central America landed on the island in 1715. Its master, Captain-General Don Juan Esteban de Ubilla was said to have buried its cargo here, in a cave. Ubilla left the island, but before he could return to get the treasure, he was killed in a violent hurricane.

Ubilla was said to have carved an S-shaped map of South America onto the cave wall where the treasure was buried.

Then, in 1761, an English pirate called Cornelius Webb turned up. He'd been sent by British Admiral Lord George Anson on a secret mission to find Ubilla's treasure. Webb found the gold, and before he left he was said to have carved the name of his boss – ANSON – into the wall of the cave. He also carved a rose because of a lovely jewelled rose that was part of the treasure.

Webb sailed off, but a terrible storm set in and broke the ship's mast, so he was forced to return to Robinson Crusoe Island. The ship now needed repairing, so he and his men set off to the nearest Chilean port for help. Before they left, they re-buried the treasure, at a location near the original cave.

A shocked Webb then discovered that his crew planned to mutiny and take the treasure for themselves! So he blew up his ship, killing everyone but himself, and escaped by rowing away in a small boat.

The Pirate Code

Blowing up the ship was certainly an explosive way for Webb to punish his crew. But betraying your captain was always a serious matter for any sailor, pirate or not.

Pirates knew that they weren't above the law. Before a voyage the pirate crew would elect a captain, and everyone would have to agree to a set of rules before they set sail.

For example:

- **No stealing** – this may sound strange, given that pirates stole for a living, but it meant that pirates couldn't steal from *each other*. Trust was vital, especially when you had valuable treasure and needed to share it out fairly
- **No fighting** – again this meant no fighting *with fellow pirates*. Best to save your energy for fighting crews of treasure-laden ships!
- **No acts of tyranny** – things like keeping a secret from the others or deserting the ship

If you broke the rules, one of the worst punishments was to be marooned on a desert island with no food or water (a bit like Selkirk). If your crime was really bad, you might even get tied up and shot. But, strangely, walking the plank was not the usual pirate punishment – that's all a bit of a myth (and a bit of a myth-tery too . . .).

Back to Webb, the only survivor of the ship – and the only person left who knew where the treasure was buried. He sent two letters back to the admiral in England, telling him the location, but Anson suddenly died and the documents were lost, never to be seen again. Webb himself died soon afterwards.

The treasure is said to contain:

 More than 800 bags of gold

 200 gold bars

21 barrels of precious stones and jewellery

 A two-foot-high gold and emerald rose

 160 chests of gold and silver coins

Treasure hunters over the years have searched high and low for it.

Pieces of Eight!

The silver coins in Webb's treasure chests were probably 'pieces of eight' – something you might have heard being shouted by a pirate, or squawked by a parrot, in a seafaring movie.

'Pieces of eight' were Spanish coins made of silver, so-called because they were worth eight Spanish reales at the time. Even more valuable were gold coins called doubloons. Any pirate would have been happy to get his hooks on either!

Also known as Spanish dollars, 'pieces of eight' were used by many different countries.

Modern Day Treasure Hunters

In 2005 a group of Chilean investigators announced that they had literally struck gold on Robinson Crusoe Island. They claimed to have found several buried barrels using a mini robot called 'Arturito'. Arturito – who had already helped solve crimes in Chile by locating buried weapons – used GPR (ground-penetrating radar) to scan the ground.

The robot was said to have found an 800-tonne hoard buried about fifteen metres down on the west side of the island. But the treasure – if it does exist – has still not been dug up! The company that owns the robot says that it is too difficult to reach and that the job is too big for them. Strange – it makes you wonder how sure they are about their find . . .

Another keen treasure hunter is an American called Bernard Keiser. He's been looking for the treasure since 1998, and is convinced that a place called Selkirk's Cave holds the key to the location. But because Robinson Crusoe Island is a protected area, he can only use basic tools such as shovels and spades. No mining or explosives are allowed (which would obviously be a lot quicker).

In 2004 Keiser and his team were excited to discover a small amount of Chinese porcelain, thought to be nearly 900 years old. Keiser believes that these pieces are just a tiny part of the treasure hoard and proof that it really exists. Other fragments, such as buttons and bits of old bottle, date from the 1600s.

Keiser is still looking, and now hopes to use new mining methods to locate the loot. Perhaps he'll strike it lucky one of these days?

The Myth of Maps

There is one thing that I'm sure Keiser, and all treasure hunters, would love to find: a treasure map! I can see it now: a furled, brown-edged roll of parchment with a skull and crossbones at the top and a drawing of a desert island. In looped, inky handwriting would be directions for finding 'X' – the spot where the treasure is buried.

Sadly, the idea that pirates made treasure maps is probably another pirate myth, a bit like walking the plank. No one has yet found an authentic map that was used by a real pirate. (Let's face it: anyone who did would have been off like a shot to find the spot.)

If you think about it, it was probably safer for a pirate to keep the secret location in his head, rather than risk drawing it on a piece of paper that could easily fall into someone else's hands. This 1883 map, drawn by a Spanish cartographer, is about the closest thing to a real treasure map you are likely to see.

An 1883 map of Cocos Island, which says that 20 expeditions have landed there to find treasure.

MY MISSION

'X' marks the spot, so they say. But how can I find pirate treasure when so many others have failed? And when there aren't any maps?

Undaunted, I'm heading for Robinson Crusoe Island to see exactly what's in Selkirk's Cave.

In 1761 Cornelius Webb found Spanish Captain Ubilla's gold hidden at this spot, inside a rocky tunnel. He used explosives to blow out the rock, creating a larger cave, before loading the treasure onto his ship. It is also where both Ubilla and Webb are said to have made their famous marks on the wall. But, most importantly, the treasure is said to have been re-buried by Webb somewhere close by . . .

Just to make the experience really authentic, I'm going to be a proper castaway for a few days. Once I've been dropped off by a fishing boat, I'll be alone on this part of the island, with only my thoughts – and, of course, a bit of kit – for company.

KIT LIST

- WATER – an essential for a desert-island castaway. If I run out, I'll collect rainwater – hope it rains . . .
- FOOD – best to avoid unknown, possibly poisonous berries and fruits. So I'll watch the local wildlife, see what they eat and follow their example

- KNIFE – I'll use it to make a spear by sharpening a pointy end of a long stick. Ideal for catching fish in shallow waters, but I'll need to move fast
- MATCHES – a fire is essential, to keep warm, for cooking, and for scaring off wild animals. If my matches get damp, I'll have to rub two sticks together instead – but that could take a very long time. A smoking fire also makes a good signal to alert passing ships and planes if I need rescue
- TORCH – to explore the dark cave (no electricity here)
- SPADE AND BAG – in case I find any treasure!
- ALEXANDER SELKIRK'S BOOK – did I mention he'd written a book? Well, he did, and it will come in very useful while exploring the island

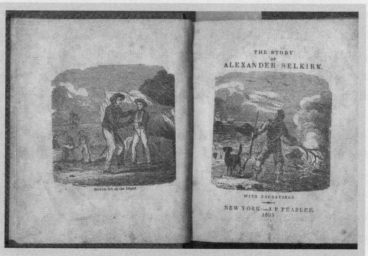

In 1713 Alexander Selkirk wrote all about his four-year island adventure.

I'm feeling pretty confident about my stay. I mean, if Alexander Selkirk managed to survive here all those years ago, I'm sure I can manage it. Selkirk only had a Bible, some clothes, a musket (an old-fashioned gun) and a few tools, including a small axe for chopping wood. When his clothes wore out, he had to wear goat-skins. In 1709 the captain of the ship that picked him up said that Selkirk looked even wilder than the island's goats! He must have looked 'furry' strange . . .

MISSION COMPLETED

My journey began with a long flight to Valparaiso, a large bustling port in Chile. From here I went by fisherman's boat to the island – a 72-hour trip on some very choppy waters. After a lot of 'ups and downs', and a few sick-bags, I was very relieved to arrive at a bay on the north of Robinson Crusoe Island – the closest place to Selkirk's Cave. The island itself looked just like a huge piece of volcanic rock jutting out from the sea, surrounded by high cliffs, and with a large mountainous peak at its centre.

At least I didn't have to build my own shelter. I made my bed for the night in the cave – a large jagged hole, about three metres high, in the side of the rock face. I spent most of the night imagining what it must have been like for Selkirk – alone here over the years, and not knowing when, if ever, he would get home again.

Using my torch, I started reading Selkirk's book. But when I got to the part where rats gnawed his feet while he was

asleep at night, I decided it was best to stop . . .

In the morning (I checked – my toes were still there!) I had a good look at the cave walls. There were lots of names and dates scratched into them, presumably made by the many visitors who've been on the island since Selkirk's day. But among them I found the carvings I was looking for: the S-shaped map, the name ANSON and a carving of a rose. Proof that Ubilla and Cornelius Webb were most definitely here. But was it proof of the treasure?

Bernard Keiser thinks so – he believes the treasure was once hidden right here, in the cave. But where? I dug hard with my spade and succeeded in making lots of very small holes. None of which had any treasure in them. The trouble is, the treasure could be anywhere – and it could be buried really deep. After two days of fruitless digging, it was time to give up and get some fresh air.

So I climbed up a steep path through thick forest to reach 'Selkirk's Lookout'. This is a high point where Alexander Selkirk used to sit and watch for passing ships, and where he eventually spotted the one that would save him.

The fishing boat returned to pick me up three days later. I was tired, hungry (spearing fish didn't work – I almost speared my foot instead) and, sadly, treasure-less.

WHAT DO YOU THINK?

1. There Is Pirate Treasure Out There Still

Legend has it that pirates always buried their treasure. But is this actually true?

People (and dogs) have always buried things that are precious to them – nothing surprising about that. In the days before banks existed, hiding your valuables was probably the best way of keeping them safe. Pirates were no different. Burying treasure on a desert island could have been just like putting money in a bank for them.

But, realistically, how many pirates would have become so rich that they were forced to bury their stash, rather than spend it all at once?

We know that some did. There's William Kidd and Gardiner's Island, and even our own Sir Francis Drake. He was the first Englishman to circumnavigate the globe, and led the English naval fleet to victory over the Spanish Armada in 1588. But you may not know that Drake was also a privateer. He and his men raided a Spanish mule train at a place called Nombre de Dios in 1572, and stole more gold and silver than they could possibly manage. So they buried it, returning a few days later to retrieve what they could, and sailed for England with their haul. Proof that burying treasure – and finding it again – can actually work . . .

History tells us that in many parts of the world piracy was,

for hundreds of years, very big business – no one really knows exactly how many pirates there were. It also tells us that pirates didn't live long lives. So why shouldn't there still be undiscovered treasure left to find? Surely treasure hunters, past and present, wouldn't have spent so much time and money looking for it if they weren't convinced that it existed.

We've looked at just a few places where pirates could have buried their treasure. But there are many, many more islands and secluded spots around the world where pirate treasure could potentially be hidden. We just need to find it!

2. Pirate Treasure Is a Myth

Would pirates really have bothered saving their treasure 'for a rainy day'? Think about it – if you were a pirate, would you have risked leaving your fortune in a hole on an island in the middle of nowhere? What were the chances of ever getting it back again? (Pretty poor, judging by the pirates we've been finding out about.)

Let's face it – pirates, by their nature, were more likely to be spenders than savers. Any stolen loot would have been divided up among the pirate crew, who would have had plenty of things to spend it on: parrots, eye-patches, peg legs . . . well, a pirate's got to look the business, hasn't he? And if you're only going to live two years, what's the point in saving?

Bear in mind too that ships of the past carried a lot of valuable cargo that couldn't actually be buried, like spices, fabrics,

tobacco and food. Pirates could easily sell or trade these items – so that's what they did.

But where did all the stories about buried treasure come from, if many weren't true?

Robert Louis Stevenson's *Treasure Island* was published in 1883; it is probably the most famous pirate adventure story ever written. It tells the story of young Jim Hawkins, who finds a treasure map and embarks on an incredible adventure involving a one-legged pirate called Long John Silver, a treasure chest, a desert island and a map. This book was so popular (and still is – find yourself a copy!) that it changed the way people think about pirates. After 1883, legends and myths about pirate treasure, islands and maps were everywhere – and have been ever since.

And perhaps that's all they are. Stories. Because if hoards of pirate treasure did exist, surely they would have been found by now?

YOU DECIDE

A-harr!! Everyone loves a swashbuckling pirate adventure. But now it's up to you to decide if real buried treasure is still there for the finding – or not. Head to the back of the book and mark your 'x' on a spot!

MYSTERY 2

The Curse of the Pharaohs

THE MISSION...

To find out if Tutankhamen's tomb had a terrible curse on it . . .

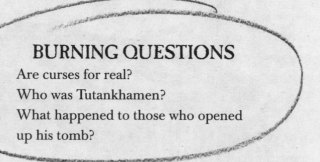

BURNING QUESTIONS

🔥 Are curses for real?

🔥 Who was Tutankhamen?

🔥 What happened to those who opened
up his tomb?

MISSION DETAILS

One of the most famous curses in history is thought to have
happened after an Englishman made a stunning discovery of
treasure. And it's sooo scary, it'll make you want your mummy!

In April 1922 Howard Carter made an amazing find. After
years of searching, he and his team finally discovered the tomb
of the ancient Egyptian pharaoh Tutankhamen.

When the underground chamber was opened up, piles of
priceless treasures were revealed. And inside a beautifully

33

decorated sarcophagus (a stone coffin) lay the mummified body of the young pharaoh, only eighteen years old when he died.

Howard Carter opens the sarcophagus – what's 'under wraps'?

Howard Carter must have thought he was the luckiest person in the world . . . but was he?

Soon afterwards, strange and sinister things began happening to some of those involved.

Could the ancient Egyptians have placed a curse upon anyone who dared to open up this precious tomb? Let's find out more . . .

THE LOCATION

Tutankhamen's tomb wasn't easy to find. It took Howard Carter five hard years of research – and a serious amount of digging – before he made his sensational discovery in a place called the Valley of the Kings, near the city of Luxor (once called Thebes) in Egypt.

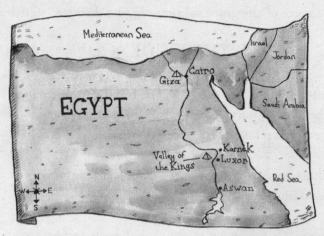

The Valley of the Kings is a large rocky valley surrounded by mountains. It was once an important burial place for the ancient Egyptians – there are more than 60 underground tombs here. Most of them have several rooms inside, connected by corridors and steps. They were made for the great pharaohs (and their families), who ruled from around 1500 to 1100 BC. Tutankhamen's tomb is one of these.

The Valley of the Kings – one of the most visited places in Egypt.

35

Thousands of people come here every year to see the tombs – and many nearby temples and ruins – at what's been called 'the world's greatest open-air museum'.

But what about Tut? Tutankhamen's body can still be seen in his original tomb, but all his lavish treasures are on display (under very high security!) at the Egyptian Museum in Cairo. No chance of any grave robbers digging their way in there . . .

THE EVIDENCE

The tomb of Tutankhamen was one of the most exciting finds of the 20th century. It is the only ancient Egyptian tomb that has ever been found intact, complete with treasures.

And no one was more excited than the man who worked so hard to find it . . .

Howard Carter was a talented and keen archaeologist who had got his very first job in Egypt in 1891, when he was just seventeen.

But it wasn't until 1917 that he got properly started on the project that was to make him famous all over the world.

At the time, most experts thought that all the tombs in the Valley of the Kings had been discovered. Not Howard Carter. He believed that there was still one more tomb to be unearthed. That of a little-known king called Tutankhamen.

But the dig would be expensive and Carter needed money to pay for it. Luckily, he found the perfect sponsor in Lord Carnarvon, who was not only wealthy, but a massive fan of Egyptology, which is, well yes, you've guessed it . . .

Carter and his team dug for five long years, looking for the missing pharaoh. By 1922 Carnarvon (and his wallet) was ready to give up, but Carter persuaded him to be patient for just a little longer.

The Big Find

The final season's excavation began. On 4 November 1922 a member of the team was digging in the sand with a stick, when he hit a stone step. Carter was immediately alerted. A day's excavation revealed the top of a flight of steps and what seemed to be a blocked entrance covered in mysterious oval stamps. Carter recognized one of them – the royal necropolis seal, showing a jackal and nine captives. Could he have finally found what he'd been searching for?

The Burial Chamber. The intact necropolis seal upon the doorway of the third funerary shrine of Tutankhamen.

Carter – though incredibly excited – calmly ordered the secret stairway to be temporarily filled in again, and quickly got in touch with Lord Carnarvon in England. Carter later wrote:

Anything, literally anything, might lie beyond that passage, and it needed all my self-control to keep from breaking down the doorway, and investigating then and there . . .
(*The Tomb of Tut-ankh-Amen* by Howard Carter, 1923)

Lord Carnarvon arrived in Egypt a few days later, and on 23 November the pair broke through the blocked doorway, revealing a passageway beyond. It was filled with rubble, all of which had to be cleared. By 26 November they had reached a second sealed door. Carter peered in, holding a flickering candle. Lord Carnarvon asked, 'Can you see anything?' – to which Carter replied: 'Yes, wonderful things!'

The incredible sight that greeted Howard Carter

Inside the 3,300-year-old antechamber of Tutankhamen's tomb lay piles of glittering golden objects – things like:

 Solid gold chariots

 Gilded animal couches – a cow, a hippo and a lion

 A golden throne, a bed, chests and chairs

 Clothes, including a leopardskin cloak with a golden head and silver claws

Two life-size statues of King Tut 'guarding' the tomb

Tut really was the King of Bling!

The objects were crammed into the room quite untidily. Historians think that Tutankhamen probably died unexpectedly, so everything was done in a bit of a rush.

In February 1923 Carter and his team finally entered the last room – the burial chamber. Inside was a massive golden shrine (like a big box). Inside that were three more shrines, then a stone sarcophagus, which in turn contained three coffins. *Phew!* It was a bit like opening a giant Egyptian pass-the-parcel!

Inside the final solid gold coffin was the mummified body of the boy-king Tutankhamen, wearing the famous gold and blue death mask

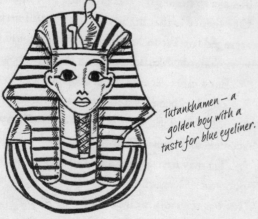

Tutankhamen – a golden boy with a taste for blue eyeliner.

The body had lain undisturbed for more than 3,000 years. Maybe it was best kept under wraps . . .

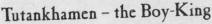

Tutankhamen – the Boy-King

Can you imagine becoming king at the age of just nine? Would you be ready to act as supreme ruler and be treated as a god on Earth? If the answer's 'yes', then you and Tutankhamen would have had a lot in common.

Tut became pharaoh (that's what they called kings in ancient Egypt) in about 1337 BC, when he was just a lad. He reigned over Egypt for nine or ten years.

Tut wasn't a particularly famous pharaoh and not that much is known about him – apart from the fact that he died at about the age of eighteen. Ah, yes – the downside to being a royal in those days (and during much of history) is that you might get murdered by a power-hungry relative who wanted your throne. Is this what happened to Tut?

Some experts think so. An X-ray of his body showed damage to his skull – was he killed by a blow to the head? One theory is that his adviser, a powerful man called Ay, arranged for Tut to be killed so that he could become the next pharaoh. 'Skullduggery' in the royal court? Ay!

But a more recent scan in 2006 showed another injury. Tut's leg had been broken just below the knee not long before he died. Some think he may have had a hunting accident and then died of an infection.

Tut may have lived a short life, but hopefully it was a good one. Given the amount of stuff he was sent off with, Tut was certainly well-prepared for whatever the afterlife had in store for him. Pharaoh-nuff, as they say!

Is this what Tut could have looked like? A modern reconstruction of his face.

Grave-robbing, Egyptian Style ...

It took months to carefully explore and excavate Tut's entire tomb. No wonder – there were a whopping 5,398 objects inside it! But why?

The ancient Egyptians believed in an afterlife, and preparing a dead person for this momentous journey to 'the other side' was very important to them.

They had to have everything they could possibly need in the next world. Things that would help them carry on living in luxury – from the best quality food and clothes to beautifully crafted furniture, chariots to get around in and beds to sleep on. All these items were placed in the tomb alongside the body. Trouble was, these things were not only useful but incredibly valuable. So, naturally, robbers tried to break in. The Egyptians did everything they could to foil the burglars:

- They used the best architects to design the tombs
- They created cunning false doorways to fool intruders
- Hidden chambers were concealed behind other rooms
- Thick slabs of stone blocked passageways
- Some think that they even placed a curse on whoever disturbed the pharaoh . . .

Unfortunately, most of these safeguards failed. From ancient times, grave robbers found ingenious ways to get into all the hidden places. Which is why all the tombs in the Valley of the Kings (apart from King Tut's) had been completely stripped of their treasures years before Howard Carter appeared on the scene.

Note: Only Very Important Dead People – pharaohs, queens, nobles, etc. – got the VIP treatment. Commoners like you and me would have been buried in the sand, with a couple of household objects, if we were lucky. Great: itchy sand and a kettle for company for all of eternity. Just as well we weren't born in ancient Egypt . . .

Even King Tut's tomb had been broken into. Evidence showed that there had been at least two attempted robberies of the tomb, probably very soon after Tutankhamen's burial. Luckily they didn't get as far as any of the really valuable stuff in the antechamber and beyond.

Did any of those grave robbers suffer the wrath of a curse? We will never know . . .

The Curse Begins . . .

Have you ever heard of the 'Curse of the Mummy'? If you think it's what your mum yells at you when you've forgotten to tidy your room – it's actually much worse (if that's possible) . . .

The mummy's alive — and it wants to relax and unwind!

The story of the Curse of the Mummy has been seen in lots of horror movies, old and modern. It goes like this:

When its ancient tomb is disturbed, a huge, hideous mummy comes to life and starts lumbering about dangerously, attacking everyone around it. With its flapping bandages (or is it toilet roll?) and beady eyes, it's really not the kind of mummy you'd want to come and tuck you up in bed at night.

However, you'll be relieved to hear that in real life there is no evidence that an Egyptian mummy has ever risen from its tomb and started threatening people. Phew . . .

But did the Egyptians have other kinds of curses, just as bad as a living mummy?

Leave my mummy alone!

The ancient Egyptians believed that if a person's body was stolen or interfered with, their spirit would not be able to return to their mummified body at night and there would be no afterlife for them.

That's why threats have been found inscribed on some tomb entrances. The punishments sounded horrible – enough to terrify anyone who dared tamper with a tomb. Take a look at this one, written in hieroglyphics on the entrance to the Third Dynasty tomb of Petety at Giza.

The gods will not allow anything to happen to me. If anyone does anything bad to my tomb, then the crocodile, hippopotamus and lion will eat him.

Imagine being eaten by a croc, a hippo and a lion – a pretty 'wild' way to go . . .

Other threats found on different tombs and statues include:

I shall seize his neck like that of a goose.
He shall die from hunger and thirst.
His relatives shall detest him.
He shall be miserable and persecuted.

I'm sure there were others. You might make up your own:

He shall stub his toe really badly on the coffee table and spill his drink.
His alarm clock shall go off at random times for the rest of his life and he shall never get a good night's sleep.
He shall forever be losing his pen just when he needs it.

I could go on . . . but I shan't because we need to get back to King Tut and his own, special curse.

The Curse of Tutankhamen

So, Tut. Was there any sign of a curse on his tomb?

Some say that the following words were inscribed in hieroglyphics by the entrance to the tomb when it was found:

They who enter this sacred tomb shall swift be visited by wings of death.

Wings of death! Sounds really scary. But strangely no trace of this 'curse' remains – it seems to have mysteriously vanished over time. Did this message ever really exist or was it just made up?

Whether it did or not, weird stuff soon started happening . . .

- Just two months after the tomb was opened, tragedy struck. In February 1923 Lord Carnarvon was bitten on the face by a mosquito and the bite became infected. He died in April

- At the moment of Lord Carnarvon's death, all the lights in Cairo – the capital city of Egypt – suddenly went out
- At the same time, in England, Carnarvon's faithful dog, Susie, let out a mournful howl – and dropped dead!
- Spookily, when Tutankhamen's mummy was finally unwrapped in 1925, it was found to have a wound on the left cheek – in exactly the same place as Lord Carnarvon's fatal insect bite! Oo-er!

Rumours began to spread of a mysterious curse, and the newspapers reported stories of a vengeful King Tut who had placed a curse upon anyone who opened the tomb. The British Museum in London was inundated with gifts of Egyptian relics from owners who were scared that they might be punished by the curse too . . .

The deaths continued. In the years following the discovery, eleven people connected with the discovery of the tomb died in strange circumstances. Among them were:

- Aubrey Herbert, Lord Carnarvon's half-brother. He died in hospital after having his teeth removed in September 1923. He had just returned from a visit to Luxor
- Lord Carnarvon's other half-brother, Captain Richard Bethell (who was also Howard Carter's personal secretary), was mysteriously found dead in his bed in November 1929

- Bethell's father, Lord Westbury, jumped to his death from the top of his apartment in February 1930
- Just four days later, Edgar Steele, the man in charge of handling the tomb artefacts at the British Museum, died in hospital following a minor operation
- Jay Gould, a businessman, visited the tomb and in 1923 died of pneumonia
- Sir Archibald Douglas-Reid, the man who X-rayed Tutankhamen's mummy, died mysteriously in 1924

But what happened to Howard Carter, the main man behind the excavation? Incredibly, he lived to the age of 65 – and never believed in curses! He stayed in Egypt, working on the excavation until 1932, then returned to London, where he spent his time touring and giving lectures about Egypt.

Other Famous Curses

What is a curse exactly? It's a kind of bad wish or spell that someone believes has been placed on an object or a person. Superstitious people might believe in curses – but how superstitious are you? Take a look at these two famous curses and see what you think:

The Hope Diamond

Beautiful, sparkling and incredibly valuable – most people would think themselves lucky to own a real diamond. But maybe not this one. The Hope Diamond is said to bring bad luck and disaster to its owner. It's a huge, deep blue diamond,

about the size of a walnut. But it's worth a bit more than your average nut – about 250 million dollars more!

The Hope Diamond has had a long history of different owners – and some have certainly had more than their fair share of bad luck:

- 🌐 The man who was said to have first stolen the diamond – Jean-Baptiste Tavernier – was later killed by wild dogs in Russia. Unlucky ...

Can a jewel really be unlucky?

- 🌐 Another owner, King Louis XVI of France (along with his queen, Marie Antoinette) lost his head in 1793 during the French Revolution. Very unlucky ...

- 🌐 A wealthy American, Evalyn McLean, bought the diamond in 1911. Her son was killed in a car crash and her daughter died at the age of 25. The family newspaper went bankrupt and Evalyn's husband later became insane. Incredibly unlucky ...

The Hope Diamond sounds a lot more hope-less than hope-ful. But why is it supposed to be cursed?

It's said that the stone was originally stolen from India, taken from the forehead or the eye of a statue of the Hindu goddess, Sita. Perhaps this is Sita's revenge for having her precious diamond taken away from her? A kind of evil eye?

The diamond was given to the Smithsonian National Museum of Natural History in Washington, DC, USA, where it is currently on display – but no one has ever offered to buy it from them ...

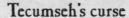

Tecumseh's curse

This curse was supposed to have been placed upon all American presidents by an angry native-American chieftain called Tecumseh. It was in revenge for being defeated by William Henry Harrison – a future US president – in the Battle of Tippecanoe, in 1811. Tecumseh was said to have sent Harrison a message saying that every 20 years an American president would die . . .

Spookily, following his prediction, seven presidents *did* die – and all of them were elected in a year ending in a zero. Each of those election years was exactly 20 years apart. Weird . . .

The seven dead presidents:

1840: **William Henry Harrison** – died from pneumonia, 1841

1860: **Abraham Lincoln** – assassinated April 1865

1880: **James Abram Garfield** – assassinated July 1881

1900: **William McKinley** – assassinated September 1901

1920: **Warren Gamaliel Harding** – died from food poisoning, 1923

1940: **Franklin Delano Roosevelt** – died from a stroke in 1945

1960: **John Fitzgerald Kennedy** – assassinated November 1963

In March 1981 President Ronald Reagan survived an assassination attempt. Some say this marked the end of the curse, as none of the presidents since then have followed the pattern.

What do you think?

MY MISSION

Probably the best way of finding out if a tomb is cursed is to:

1. Open up an Egyptian tomb; then . . .
2. See if a terrible fate befalls me.

BUT this idea falls down in two very important places. Firstly, I don't think there are many, if any, Egyptian tombs left for me to find. Secondly, even if there were, I'd be more than a bit nervous about breaking open that sealed doorway. I mean, what if ancient Egyptian curses do exist? Being eaten by a croc, a hippo and a lion isn't likely to happen in my neck of the woods (unless the local zoo has a break-out), but you never know . . .

So, instead, I'm going to the place where there are more ancient Egyptian tombs than you can shake a stick at. The Valley of the Kings, of course. I'll get to see the real Tutankhamen's tomb for myself. And see if the atmosphere feels, well, cursed in any way . . .

KIT LIST

- LARGE BOTTLE OF WATER – essential in a hot, dry climate
- HIGH-FACTOR SUN-BLOCK AND SUN HAT – there are no shady trees here to shelter under
- STURDY TRAINERS – many of the tombs have crumbly, uneven surfaces and steps – it would be easy to take a tumble. And I don't want to end up with a broken leg – that would be spookily like King Tut!

- A HEAD TORCH – it can be pretty dark in some of the tombs and I'll need to see where I'm going – and have my hands free in case I stumble
- A PEN AND NOTEBOOK – for taking notes of any interesting hieroglyphics I might come across
- A TUTANKHAMEN HISTORY BOOK – would be useful
- CAMERA WITH A FLASH – for taking shots in those dark chambers

MISSION COMPLETED

Wow. Egypt was hot. Really hot! Temperatures here can reach 120° Fahrenheit (49° Celsius). So I had to get going very early in the morning, before the heat got too much. My visit to Tutankhamen's tomb started with an alarm call at 5 a.m.

The entrance to the tomb would have been easy to miss – it's just a plain rectangular doorway cut into the rock. Once inside, you walk through a narrow passageway and turn right into the antechamber. It looked very different from when Howard Carter first found it – there are no heaps of glittering treasure here any more, just a bare room. All the tomb's riches have long since gone to the Egyptian Museum in Cairo.

Then it was straight on to the burial chamber. Inside, it was hot, humid and packed with people desperate to get a glimpse of the famous pharaoh. The room was small, with beautiful golden walls covered in paintings of Egyptian figures and animals. In the middle, protected by glass, lay King Tut himself.

Here lies King Tut.

It was all super-spooky. The small, dark chamber. The mummified corpse of Tutankhamen, who had been lying here for more than 3,000 years. I nervously wondered if he might rise up out of his sarcophagus for a quick 'coffin break'. Yes, I've definitely been watching too many 'Curse of the Mummy' horror movies . . . but now that I've seen a real Egyptian mummy, I can see why they make such good subjects!

Despite my nerves, I survived my visit – no signs of any strange infections or lights going out, or anything else weird. And I feel very lucky to have seen the real King Tut because he won't be here for much longer. Tut is a really popular guy – he gets up to a thousand visitors a day! And that's the problem. If all those people carry on tramping through the most popular tomb in town, there won't be much left of it in a few years' time. To stop the damage, Tut's tomb will soon be closed to the public, but an exact replica is being made for visitors to see at the Valley of the Kings.

WHAT DO YOU THINK?

1. The Curse of Tutankhamen Doesn't Exist

Yes, people *did* die after the tomb was discovered – but maybe those people would have died anyway? If the tomb really had been cursed, surely everyone present would have died or had something awful happen to them?

Let's look at the facts. There were 22 people present when the tomb was first opened in 1922 – and by 1934 only six of them had died. There were just ten people there when Tut's mummy was finally unwrapped – and none of them died very soon afterwards.

There's no doubt that Lord Carnarvon's death was very strange. But was it all just a coincidence? The story of all the lights going out in Cairo at the moment of his death is true, but if you've ever visited Cairo, you'll know that blackouts do happen – and in the 1920s the electricity supply was even more unreliable than it is now.

And what about Howard Carter? As the main leader of the expedition and the first to enter the tomb, he should have been a prime target for Tut's revenge. But he lived to the age of 65.

Howard Carter himself never believed in a curse (if he had, he probably wouldn't have chosen a career as an Egyptian archaeologist!). And there has never been any writing found on Tut's tomb that resembles a curse, despite the story of the spooky 'wings of death' inscription found on the entrance,

which could easily have been made up by the press.

Some experts say that Egyptian curses simply don't exist. They think that tomb inscriptions were just messages meant to frighten off enemies. They believe that all the stories of cursed mummies were made up by newspapers and films in the West to frighten audiences. If that's true, it worked!

2. The Tombs Are Toxic

There could be another reason to explain why some people who visited Egyptian tombs got sick, or even died. Some experts think that there could be dangerous bacteria inside them. But how did it get there?

As well as treasures, the Egyptians put food, plants and other living things into the tombs. These items would have decayed, creating a perfect breeding ground for bacteria. And once the tombs were opened up, the bacteria could have escaped, making people close by really ill.

It's also possible that the Egyptians deliberately poisoned their tombs to defend them from intruders.

The ancient Egyptians certainly knew their poisons. They extracted toxic substances from all kinds of plants, minerals, animals and insects. It's possible that they placed these lethal poisons inside the tombs, waiting to wreak havoc on anyone who disturbed the sleeping pharaoh. Experts say that some poisons can live for hundreds of years if they are sealed up in a space with no light or air.

BUT if the poisonous air was to blame, wouldn't all the people present at the opening of a tomb have got sick in some way? And that didn't happen with Tut's tomb.

3. The Curse Is Real!

If you think that Tutankhamen's curse is real, firstly you have to believe that curses exist. Secondly, you have to believe that Egyptians cursed their tombs.

We know that the Egyptians believed in magic. They called it 'heka' and thought it was the magical force responsible for creating their world. Heka was used by most Egyptians, from the lowly to the noble.

Imagine a world where priests perform magical rituals to protect the pharaoh, scorpion-charmers use magic to get rid of poisonous creatures, and nurses use magic to heal the sick. People called 'protection-makers' offer you amulets – small, magical objects to wear or carry for protection.

Some of this magic was used to try and harm others. Historians know that Egyptian ceremonies were performed to curse enemies. Drawings of enemy gods were stamped on, burned, then dissolved in buckets of urine!

A baboon to protect you – one of many different kinds of Egyptian amulet.

The names of human enemies were written on clay pots or figures and then burned, broken or buried.

The ancient Egyptians did everything they could to protect their precious tombs. If they went to all the trouble of building hidden rooms and blocking up doorways, mightn't they have used their magic to put a curse on the intruders too?

You might also think that the deaths following Tut's discovery prove that the curse was real. Some of the ways in which the people died were indeed strange and mysterious. Even stranger is the tale of Susie the terrier who, thousands of miles away at the Carnarvon family home, dropped down dead at the very moment when Lord Carnarvon died in Egypt. How can anyone explain that?

Many people around the world seem to believe in curses – but are you one of them? Turn to the end of the end of the book and cast your vote!

YOU DECIDE

Do you think that an ancient curse caused the deaths of those associated with Tut? Or do you think that all curses are just made-up nonsense, invented to scare superstitious people. It's your call!

The *Legend of El Dorado*

THE MISSION ...

... to find out if the legendary kingdom of El Dorado really exists ...

BURNING QUESTIONS

🔥 Where is El Dorado?

🔥 Why is everyone so desperate to find it?

🔥 Is it real – or imaginary?

MISSION DETAILS

A city of glittering gold. Sparkling jewels, and riches beyond your wildest dreams ...

This is El Dorado. Hopeful treasure hunters have spent years looking for it – and some have even lost their lives during their quest. How hard would you try to find a place like this?

Treasure hunters dream of such a golden opportunity ...

The mystery of El Dorado began in the sixteenth century, when explorers from Spain began arriving on the coasts of Central and South America. There was a lot to conquer – a massive continent, which they called the 'New World'.

The explorers soon realized that the New World, with its vast resources of gold and silver, could make them very rich and powerful. So when they heard about a legendary ceremony that involved throwing away piles of precious gold and jewels, their ears pricked up. Treasure for the taking? *'Si, señor!'*

The ceremony was supposed to take place near a mountain lake, where a local tribe called the Muisca welcomed a new chief by covering him in a sticky substance, then showering him in pure golden dust. Like a precious golden statue, the chief would drift out onto the water on a raft. They named him El Dorado – 'the gilded one'.

El Dorado would then jump into the lake, washing off the golden dust, accompanied by cheers and shouts. 'Water' way to celebrate!

Then – and this was the really interesting part for the Spaniards – piles of jewels and treasures were thrown into the water as a gift to their lake-dwelling god.

From this ritual, rumours grew of an entire kingdom awash with gold and other precious treasures.

The legend of El Dorado has survived for hundreds of years – but the real El Dorado has never been found . . .

THE LOCATION

Lake Guatavita can be found high up in the Andes mountains, about 50 kilometres from bustling Bogotá, the capital city of modern-day Colombia.

The circular lake lies inside a crater, which was created by a massive meteorite strike about 2,000 years ago. The Muisca knew nothing of meteorites. They believed the almighty bang was caused by the arrival of the sun god, who then made his home at the bottom of the lake. Must have been a really 'deep' guy . . .

THE EVIDENCE

The Spanish first heard the story of El Dorado from native South Americans they had captured. These tales were backed up by others, like Colombian writer Juan Rodríguez Freyle, who in 1636 wrote:

By that lake of Guatavita they made a great raft of reeds, decorating it as beautifully as they could . . . They undressed the heir, anointed him with a sticky earth and dusted him with ground and powdered gold, so that he went in the raft completely covered with this metal. The golden Indian made his offering, casting all the gold and emeralds he had brought into the middle of the lake . . .

The guy on the right is blowing golden dust over the new chief. Bet there were lots of volunteers to sweep up afterwards!

It didn't take the Spanish long to find the lavish lake of legend. But getting the treasure out of the lake was another matter (this was way before scuba-diving had been thought of). The only way was to drain the lake of water – but how?

Draining Disasters

In 1545 two conquistadors and a large group of workers used 'buckets' made from hollowed-out gourds (a sort of large fruit) to scoop water from the lake. They must have done some serious scooping because, amazingly, they managed to lower the water level by three metres! It took them three months – but their super-scooping was in vain. A little gold was found, but nothing like the riches they had imagined

In 1578 treasure hunter Antonio de Sepúlveda had a better idea. Why not cut a huge chunk of earth out of the rim of the lake and lower the water level that way? Great idea, Antonio! He went ahead, but the earthworks collapsed and many workers were killed. Again, only a small amount of gold was found

In 1898 a group of 'experts' from London dug a tunnel which opened up in the centre of the lake. Success! Most of the water drained away. But it left behind a deep, sticky mud that was too sludgy to investigate – by the next day, the mud had been baked solid by the hot sun. Finding a mere £500 worth of gold, the Londoners gave up. And the lake soon filled again

Several other attempts were made over the years using mechanical earth movers, but nothing much was found. It almost seemed as if the God Who Lived in the Lake didn't want anyone to find his treasure; treasure which could have looked like this:

The beautiful raft of legend . . . definitely worth its weight in gold.

This raft was found inside a Muisca clay jar, hidden in a cave south of Bogotá, in 1969. It shows the El Dorado ceremony in action. Are there more treasures like this to be found?

The Truth about the Conquistadors

The European explorers called the Americas the 'New World'. Which came as a bit of a surprise to the many people already living there – it wasn't exactly 'new' to them!

Christopher Columbus had arrived here in 1492, and he was followed in the sixteenth and seventeenth centuries by Spanish explorers – called 'conquistadors' –

eager to conquer these lands. But native South Americans had been living on the continent for many hundreds of years before the Europeans arrived – and changed everything.

- Many conquistadors saw the locals as savages, and exploited them, robbing their towns and villages and taking their treasures. Battles sometimes broke out between the Europeans and the American Indians, but local bows and arrows were no match for smoking Spanish guns

- The Spanish wanted to change the locals' religion. They brought priests with them, so that they could persuade the natives to become Catholics, just like them

- The arrival of the explorers brought other deadly consequences – diseases like measles and flu. The locals had never had these illnesses before, and thousands died. Some experts think that 90 per cent of the population were killed by European diseases

Between them, the Spanish, closely followed by the Portuguese, colonized much of South and Central America. They became rulers and were incredibly powerful in the region for more than 400 years. (The English, meanwhile, were busy colonizing many other parts of the world, including North America.)

Stories like that of El Dorado encouraged Europeans to journey further into the continent to find as much gold as possible. Were they adventurous explorers – or greedy invaders?

A Change of Location

So – if the treasure of El Dorado wasn't at the bottom of Lake Guatavita – where was it?

The search eventually moved from Colombia to Venezuela and Guyana in the east.

Rumours began spreading that El Dorado could be found much further east. After the lake fiasco, the Spanish turned their attention to the eastern foothills of the Andes, and several explorers set out to see what they could find. Including a particularly famous conquistador called Gonzalo Pizarro.

Pizarro – finding El Dorado would certainly have been a feather in his cap ...

Pizarro's quest

Pizarro was living in Ecuador when he heard a story told by the locals about a wonderful place full of gold and spices that could be found in the mountains of the east. Here lived a tribe so rich that they covered their chief in gold. Believing it was the fabled El Dorado, Pizarro went east in 1541. He didn't exactly travel light, taking with him:

- Hundreds of Spanish soldiers
- About 4,000 native South Americans
- 4,000 pigs (for food)
- Horses, dogs and llamas (for carrying supplies)
- A large river ship called a brigantine
- His friend and lieutenant, Francisco de Orellana
- . . . And the kitchen sink (just joking)

Despite all this preparation, the expedition didn't go well. The going was really tough and many of the men died along the way from disease and attacks by unfriendly locals.

Orellana and a few men sailed down the river in search of food but never returned (apparently Orellana's men wouldn't let him turn back because they didn't want to share the food they had found with the others!).

Incredibly, Orellana eventually ended up discovering the mighty Amazon river and becoming the first known person to travel down its entire length! Despite this great achievement, he never found El Dorado – and neither did Pizarro.

Martínez and Manoa

But more rumours were emerging about El Dorado's location. In 1542 a Spaniard called Juan Martínez told his strange story. He had been part of an expedition that went off with a bang when their supply of gunpowder accidentally exploded. Martínez got the blame, and his punishment was to be tied up and set adrift in a boat on a river. Presumably to a watery end . . .

Martínez would probably have died, had he not been captured by a group of locals. He said he was then blindfolded and marched for four days to an unknown location. When his blindfold was taken off, he found himself in an incredible city, full of houses made of shining gold and precious stones. He was taken to a palace and met the king, who was called El Dorado. Just like the story, El Dorado was bathed with gold dust every day.

Martínez begged for his freedom; El Dorado refused at first, but later changed his mind and set him free. The Spaniard eventually managed to get to the city of Margarita, where he told everyone his incredible tale. It was indeed incredible – and to this day no one knows whether he made the whole thing up or not.

Martínez was convinced that the city he had been taken to was called Manoa, on the shores of a great lake named Parima. Parima was then part of Guyana, in north-east South America.

An ancient map shows the location of Manoa – but did it ever exist?

Manoa became the next hot spot for El Dorado hunters, and the Spanish mounted five major expeditions to find it.

Going for Gold

The quest for gold was tough – with soaring mountains, steamy rainforests and huge plains to cross – but Pizarro, and others like him, didn't mind risking their lives on dangerous expeditions. They had a taste for treasure – and they wanted more.

They were inspired by another Spanish explorer, Hernán Cortés, who had already defeated the mighty Aztecs in what is

now Mexico. Pizarro, who'd set out from Spain in 1530, went on to do a similar thing in South America, battling the Inca of Peru.

The Inca Empire was huge, dominating the mountains of the Andes for about 4,000 kilometres, all the way from the coast to the Amazonian rainforest. The Incas ruled over more than 12 million people. But it took just two years for Pizarro and his men to defeat them and take their gold and silver, using some underhand tactics along the way.

The sneaky Spanish arranged a meeting with a powerful Inca emperor called Atahualpa. But they kidnapped him and demanded a huge ransom of gold, equivalent to millions of pounds today. Once they got the gold, instead of setting Atahualpa free, as they had promised, they killed him. The Spanish then invaded Cuzco, the most important city of the Inca Empire.

One of the first Spaniards to enter Cuzco couldn't believe his eyes at the sight of so much gold. He described seeing decorations, figurines, animals, vases, pots, jewellery – everything seemed to be made of gold!

'They had also a garden, the clods of which were made of pieces of fine gold; and it was artificially sown with golden maize, the stalks, as well as the leaves and cobs, being of that metal.'

No wonder the Spanish got a taste for treasure. And a real determination to find El Dorado . . . whatever it took.

Raleigh – Truth or Myth?

It wasn't only the Spanish who wanted gold. You're sure to have heard of Sir Walter Raleigh. (No, he didn't invent the bicycle ...)

Raleigh was actually a famous English courtier and explorer. He was also a great favourite of the powerful Queen Elizabeth I.

There are a few good stories about him. But which ones are true? See what you think:

STORY – Sir Walter Raleigh once laid his fine cloak over a muddy puddle so that Queen Elizabeth wouldn't have to get her royal toes dirty. What a gentleman!

Sir Walter – so 'frilled' to meet you!

TRUTH – Though this kind of thing probably happened to her all the time, sadly it never happened with Sir Walter. The cloak-and-puddle story is a myth, one that was probably made up by a historian called Thomas Fuller, who was known for 'exaggerating'.

STORY – Following one of his expeditions, Sir Walter brought the first potato back to England. It's been one of the nation's favourite vegetables ever since.

TRUTH – He didn't. Potatoes were introduced to Europe by the Spanish, and they gradually became popular throughout the continent, and in Britain. But they are still one of the nation's favourite veggies.

But one thing people don't generally know about Sir Walter – and this one is actually true – is that he believed in the legend of El Dorado. So much so that he organized, at huge expense, two expeditions to South America in search of the fabled treasure.

Sir Walter really wanted to impress good Queen Bess (well, who wouldn't?). So in 1595 he left England, taking five ships with him. He had a plan. He would sail to the island of Trinidad, leave the ships there, then travel to the mainland of Guyana in smaller boats and sail along the Orinoco river to find the legendary city of Manoa.

Raleigh and his men got as far as the Orinoco river but then gave up. They had some good excuses. The conditions were terrible, the rainy season was starting (and we're not just talking drizzle – this is the rainforest, remember!). Also, the Spanish were dangerously close behind them.

But Sir Walter's dream didn't end there. In 1617 he set sail again, this time with fourteen ships and about 1,000 men, including his son, Walt. Most of the men got as far as the Orinoco river. But the Spanish (who weren't very happy about the Brits being on their territory) caught up with them and during the fighting Raleigh's son was killed.

The English searched in vain for about two months, all the while fending off Spanish attacks. They found nothing, and Sir Walter returned home a sad and dejected man, with only one ship left and deserted by many of his men. Because he had breached the conditions of his Royal Charter, once home, Sir Walter was imprisoned and sent for trial.

In 1618 he was executed at the Tower of London under the order of King James (Queen Elizabeth had died in 1603). Raleigh apparently asked to see the axe that would cut off his head and said:

'This is sharp medicine ... that will cure all my diseases.'

A bit of an understatement – but he seemed to take his punishment well ...

To the very end, Sir Walter still thought that El Dorado existed. Like the cast of *Glee*, he just never stopped believin'.

Four hundred years later, and we have to ask: *Did the gold of El Dorado even exist in the first place?*

In his 1849 poem 'El Dorado', writer Edgar Allan Poe summed up the problem:

> Gaily bedight,
> A gallant knight,
> In sunshine and in shadow,
> Had journeyed long,
> Singing a song,
> In search of Eldorado.
>
> But he grew old –
> This knight so bold –
> And o'er his heart a shadow
> Fell as he found
> No spot of ground
> That looked like Eldorado.

MY MISSION

Those looking for an 'El Dorado' don't have to go too far these days:

- 🌐 There are towns called El Dorado in Venezuela, Mexico, Argentina, Canada and Peru
- 🌐 El Dorado International Airport is located in Colombia
- 🌐 But the place with the most El Dorados is the USA – at least thirteen states have a town named after the legendary city!

Finding the real El Dorado is going to be much, much harder. I'm going to follow in Sir Walt's steps (hopefully, without losing my head) and see if I can locate the lost city of Manoa. Martínez said it was on a salt lake called Lake Parime, close to the Orinoco river in what is now Venezuela.

It's a long, long journey, starting with a flight to the massively big and busy Venezuelan city of Caracas. From there, a twelve-hour bus trip takes me to the banks of the Orinoco, where I will board a small canoe to make my way downriver. 'Orinoco' (apart from being the name of a Womble – ask your parents!) actually means 'a place to paddle' – and I'll certainly be doing a lot of that. But as it is one of the longest rivers in South America (2,140 km), I won't be attempting its entire length . . .

I won't be having a refreshing swim either, despite the heat. Apparently there are electric eels (shocking!) and piranha, who might just fancy a bite . . .

I'd prefer to come back intact, ready to take on more mysteries!

KIT LIST

A large part of the Orinoco river flows through steamy, humid rainforest and mangrove swamp. I'll need to be fully prepared:

 LIGHTWEIGHT FIBREGLASS CANOE AND PADDLES – with space to store all my supplies

 TENT AND HAMMOCK – I'll need to sleep raised above the rainforest floor because of all the insects, scorpions and snakes . . .

 A GOOD MOSQUITO NET – there'll be hundreds of mosquitoes around at dusk and dawn

 EXTRA-STRONG INSECT REPELLENT – those pesky mozzies again, plus a whole variety of other biting insects. Repellent spray should make them buzz off!

 CAMERA AND BINOCULARS

 COMPASS – the rainforest is huge and you can easily get lost if you wander off route. And there's not much chance of being found if you do . . .

 HEAD TORCH – it's pitch dark in the jungle at night

SWISS ARMY KNIFE WITH ATTACHMENTS – will come in handy for lots of jobs

 SUN HAT/SUN-SCREEN/SUN-BLOCK

 WATER-PURIFICATION TABLETS/WATER BOTTLE/FOOD

 JUNGLE SURVIVAL GUIDE – full of useful tips for rainforest survival

MISSION COMPLETED

I'm sweaty, hot and tired – after paddling thousands of metres in a canoe, I'm now wondering why I didn't use the motorized version . . .

But the long journey was brightened up by the most amazing wildlife, bringing a smile to my sweaty face. Creatures like giant river otters, howler monkeys, brightly coloured parrots and toucans. Not all the wildlife was welcoming, though. Large caymans (a sort of croc) and river pythons got me paddling as fast as I could in the other direction!

But the best sight of all had to be the pink river dolphins. Yes, pink dolphins! These friendly freshwater dolphins have long snouts and are found in very few places in the world – but luckily the Orinoco river is one of them. A friendly pod (that's the name for a group of dolphins) popped their heads out of the water to investigate my canoe.

But what about El Dorado? There are now lots of towns and villages close to the Orinoco river that didn't exist in Walter Raleigh's day. (The journey would have been much, much harder then.) Which meant that there were quite a few people around to talk to. I spoke to lots of friendly locals on the river banks, but no one I met along the way had heard of the town of Manoa. There was no sign of it. Some ancient maps show the lake – but were these made up by explorers? I just don't know.

WHAT DO YOU THINK?

1. El Dorado Is a Myth

Could El Dorado be just a story? But if so, why have so many people risked their lives to find it? It's a myth-tery!

Perhaps the rumours got out of control. The Muisca tribe's ancient tradition of throwing treasure into a lake is well-known. But did the Europeans' greed for gold make them imagine more? Perhaps they were so dazzled by the riches of the Aztecs and the Incas that they persuaded themselves that there must be more wealth out there. The kingdom of El Dorado fitted the bill perfectly.

There is another possibility. Maybe the native Americans made up a lot of the stories about El Dorado. But why?

As you know by now, the Spanish conquistadors weren't exactly popular with the locals. Think about it: what would you do if you were faced with a bunch of strange people with guns arriving at your village and demanding information

about a 'golden kingdom'? You could tell them that El Dorado didn't exist – and risk their anger. Or you could tell them what they wanted to hear. Inventing a fictional city and telling the Spanish it was hundreds of kilometres away from your own village would have been a sure-fire way of getting rid of the annoying intruders. Hopefully for a very, very long time . . .

We know that old-fashioned adventurers weren't able to find El Dorado. And modern-day explorers – with all the GPS technology that they didn't have hundreds of years ago – haven't been able to find it either. Does that tell us that it never actually existed?

2. El Dorado Exists

Some people think it's likely that there was indeed a golden city full of treasures. The Inca were fabulously wealthy – the richest civilization anywhere in South America. (At least, they were until the Spanish arrived . . .)

The Incas mined gold and silver and used it for decorating buildings, making statues and crafting many beautiful treasures. The city of Cuzco, in Peru, boasted a golden palace, temples with roofs of gold, even a golden fountain. But their love of gold wasn't just about money; gold was the sign of their sun god and symbolized his power. Golden objects were used for offerings to the gods.

Sadly, many of these precious treasures were taken by the Europeans and melted down to be made into gold bars. But was all of it?

Some people believe that groups of Incas may have run away and set up their own hidden empire in a secret location, filled with riches that they had taken with them. Deep in the rainforest or high up in the mountains would have been an ideal place to hide. Perhaps Manoa was the Incas' hidden city? Or maybe there is another secret kingdom somewhere?

The area of South America we are talking about is vast, with thousands of kilometres of unexplored rainforest. Even now, archaeologists are still finding new evidence of ancient hidden civilizations deep in the jungle. The golden kingdom hasn't yet been found – but this doesn't mean its remains aren't out there somewhere . . .

We also know that European explorers on the Orinoco river did see Indian traders carrying gold, jewellery and other precious items. They said the goods came from Manoa – but the actual location of this place was never revealed.

The Spanish were convinced that there was a hidden city that the locals were keeping from them. Were they right?

YOU DECIDE

'Looking for El Dorado' describes someone who is searching for their life's great wish or ambition, but who has never found it. Will we ever find the real El Dorado? You must decide . . .

The
Crystal Skull Conundrum

THE MISSION ...

... to find out if an ancient civilization made mysterious crystal skulls ...

BURNING QUESTIONS

🔥 How were the skulls made?
🔥 Are they all fakes?
🔥 Do crystal skulls have supernatural powers?

MISSION DETAILS

Have you ever seen a crystal skull? It's a beautiful but spooky-looking thing – a realistic human skull carved from sparkling quartz crystal.

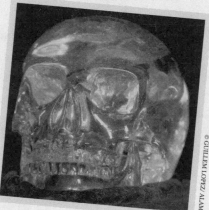

© GUILLEM LÓPEZ/ALAMY

People have always been fascinated by these skulls. Some believe they possess strange supernatural forces: even the power to heal – or to curse ...

Do all crystal skulls have a glassy-eyed stare?

A few think that the skulls might even have come from the legendary island of Atlantis (if it ever existed) or that they were brought to Earth by alien visitors!

But what do the experts think? At one time most of them thought that the skulls were made by the Aztecs or the Mayans, hundreds of years ago. But now there is a big debate over the skulls' origins and exactly how they were made. Are they bony phoneys – or the real deal?

It's time to delve deeper into the strange, sparkling world of crystal skulls . . .

THE LOCATION

To see a crystal skull for yourself, you'd have to visit one of the world's great cities. There are three famous skulls currently on display in museums in London, Washington DC, and Paris. The rest are in the hands of private owners around the world.

You may even spot a crystal skull in a shop window when you're out and about, but don't get too excited if you do. There are plenty of souvenirs around that are just copies of the original skulls, mostly made from glass.

THE EVIDENCE

A skull might not be the first thing you'd think of putting on display in your bedroom (except maybe at Halloween), but some civilizations thought differently.

Skulls were really important to several of the ancient peoples of Central America (often called Mesoamerica by historians). The Aztec god of death Mictlantecuhtli (try saying that really quickly) was shown as a skeleton or a person wearing a skull. The Mayans and the Aztecs liked to build structures called skull racks – a gruesome 'wall' of skulls! Some racks were made of real skulls belonging to battle victims and unfortunate locals sacrificed to the gods. Others were carved of stone.

I bet the ancients 'racked' their brains to think of this idea ...

Skull patterns were used to decorate shrines and temples, and colourful masks were made from real human skulls inlaid with turquoise and jade.

Human skulls were sometimes used for religious rituals. In 2012 a hoard of 50 skulls was found buried near Mexico City, thought to have come from human sacrifices more than 1,000 years ago – it's enough to chill you to the bone . . .

And if you visit Mexico today, you'll see that skulls are still really popular – in art, festivals and architecture. (Though, you'll

An Aztec skull mask – note the real teeth. You could wear it to a party but there'd be no body to go with . . .

be relieved to hear, no longer for human sacrifices.) Mexican kids can even eat tiny sugar skulls from the sweet shop – mmm, crunchy!

Mexicans celebrate the Day of the Dead to remember their loved ones. Check out this bunch of boneheads!

The crystal skulls we're talking about are supposed to be very special. Many believe that they were made by either the Aztecs or the Mayans. But who were these people, exactly?

Pyramids, Sacrifices and Deadly Ball Games

Civilizations such as the Aztecs, the Mayans, and others, once lived in a region called Mesoamerica, which includes parts of Mexico, Guatemala, Belize, Honduras and El Salvador.

The Mayans lived mainly in the rainforests of the Yucatán peninsula of Mexico from around 900 BC. Their civilization peaked around 300 AD – the height of their achievements in art, learning and culture. But then, mysteriously, they began to abandon their cities. Some think the forests couldn't support so many people. Others blame war or drought. Whatever happened, by 800 AD the Mayans had all but disappeared . . .

The Aztecs lived in central Mexico from the fourteenth to the sixteenth century, eventually ruling over a huge empire under their leader, Montezuma. They built an impressive capital city called Tenochtitlán (now Mexico City). In 1519 the Spanish conquistadors, led by Hernán Cortés, attacked the Aztec Empire. The Aztecs were on their way out . . .

A mighty Aztec warrior 'wings' it!

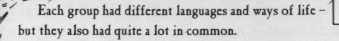

Each group had different languages and ways of life – but they also had quite a lot in common.

🌐 Both Aztecs and Mayans ruled large, powerful empires

🌐 They worshipped many different gods and made sacrifices to keep them happy. Animals, birds and insects were often used as offerings at religious ceremonies. And sometimes human beings too . . .

🌐 They built amazing cities, temples and stone pyramids, used for religious ceremonies. You can still see their ruins today – many tourists visit these ancient sites to marvel at them

Marvelling at the Chichén Itzá stepped pyramid in Mexico.

© JAN COBB PHOTOGRAPHY LTD /GETTY IMAGES

🌐 They played a notorious ball game, in which you had to try and get a rubber ball through a ring without using your hands or feet. Players used hips, thighs and upper arms in an attempt at 'keepy-uppy'. Sound like fun? You wouldn't have been laughing if you'd been the leader of the losing side. He would probably have his head cut off (remember that skull rack from earlier?). Losing doesn't get any tougher than this . . .

An ancient ball court today. Could you get a ball through that ring without using your hands?

Yes, we know quite a lot about the Aztecs and the Mayans. But nowhere have historians found evidence that they made crystal skulls. Or what they would have been used for. Maybe they were just beautiful works of art – or perhaps they had more significance?

The Legend of the Thirteen Skulls

Some people believe that there are just thirteen real crystal skulls in existence. They think that the skulls have incredible powers – but only if they are all brought together in a certain way.

Twelve of the skulls must be arranged in a circle and the largest, thirteenth, skull placed in the middle. When this happens, it is said that the skulls will have the combined power and wisdom that humankind needs to survive the future. Impressive!

But, confusingly, some people believe the complete opposite – that if all thirteen crystal skulls are gathered together, it will bring about the end of the world! No wonder no one's ever tried it . . .

Thirteen – a lucky or unlucky number when it comes to the skulls?

It's All Over – or Is It?

Talking of the end of the world, chances are you'll remember a certain date – Friday 21 December 2012. It was memorable because this was the day some people believed our world would come to an end. And it was all because of the ancient Mayans.

The Mayans were good at maths and astronomy and they devised advanced calendar systems. And it just so happened that their calendar ended on 21 December 2012.

Some took this as a 'sign' that everything was over for the human race! When the fateful day arrived, they were probably hiding under their tables waiting for a meteorite to strike the Earth – but nothing happened. I guess the believers are all feeling a bit silly now . . .

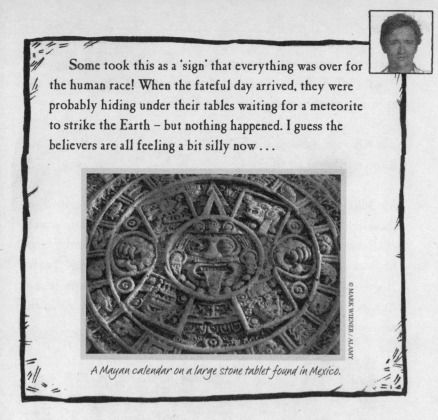

A Mayan calendar on a large stone tablet found in Mexico.

Is it too far-fetched to believe that a few pieces of crystal could contain enough power to save – or end – our world?

One crystal skull was thought to be so powerful, it was said to bring nothing but unhappiness to those around it . . .

The Skull of Doom

Actually called the Mitchell-Hedges skull (but let's face it, the 'Skull of Doom' sounds much more exciting), this skull has had a spooky reputation for years. It was owned by a man called Frederick Mitchell-Hedges, who claimed it had evil powers that were once unleashed by Mayan priests to strike people dead. Other stories have said that it emits blue lights from its eyes and crashes computer hard drives!

But where did the doom-laden skull come from? And how did its owner know all this?

Mr Mitchell-Hedges was a proper old-fashioned explorer who travelled the world in the early 1900s, seeking adventure and challenge (sounds right up my street). On this particular trip he was accompanied by his teenage daughter, Anna. Their story – which sounds like something out of an Indiana Jones movie – starts when the pair began investigating the ruins of an ancient Mayan temple in Belize.

F. A. Mitchell-Hedges with a group of Chucunaque Indians. And a pipe.

According to Anna, she noticed something shining through a crack in a pyramid and alerted her father.

Unable to reach the object, the pair returned to the spot the following day, but it took a long while to move enough stones to make a decent-sized opening at the top of the pyramid. An apprehensive Anna was then lowered inside. She later said:

With two ropes tied around my body and a light strapped to my head, I was lowered into the darkness, terrified of the snakes and scorpions that might be down there.

This definitely sounds like a movie – perhaps Indi-Anna Jones!

Anna said she saw a shining object, which she grabbed and wrapped in her shirt. Once in the light, she could see that it was a transparent skull, made of crystal, heavy, and about two-thirds the size of a real skull. It had a moveable, detachable jaw, unlike other crystal skulls that have been found.

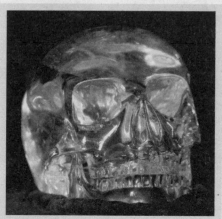

The Skull of Doom – as evil as it looks?

© GUILLEM LOPEZ / ALAMY

The crystal skull made the pair famous. Mr M-H even wrote a book about it. He claimed that it was made by at least five generations of Mayans, who had slowly shaped it out of a piece of rock crystal by painstakingly rubbing it down with sand. (We have no idea how he knew this, as he couldn't possibly have been there at the time . . .)

But some think that our intrepid explorer had an over-active imagination. Around that time there happened to be a popular adventure story called *The Crystal Skull*. It featured a spooky skull stolen by a character called Lyndon Cromer, an academic who robbed ancient sites to get his hands on precious artefacts.

A suspicious-looking Lyndon Cromer turns headhunter . . .

Was Frederick Mitchell-Hedges 'inspired' by this novel to come up with an equally exciting story about his own crystal skull?

We'll never know – but there are certainly those who disagree with the Mitchell-Hedgeses' version of events. Some say that their story just doesn't stand up. There were no photographs and no witnesses, so we only have their word for it.

Moreover, Anna Mitchell-Hedges has always been very unclear about the actual date of the find. It was sometime in the mid-1920s, but she can't remember exactly when . . . Also her story of being lowered down into a pyramid on a rope does sound a bit like a movie, rather than real life. Does it all sound rather suspicious to you?

Many people would say so. They think that the skull might have been bought from a London art dealer in October 1943 – years later than it was said to have been found.

Anna later toured the world giving private viewings of the 'Skull of Doom'. It made her and her father famous – but only they knew the real truth about where it came from . . .

Skulls – Fakes or Finds?

So, what's the latest verdict on the other crystal skulls?

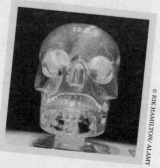

- London, England: For years the British Museum believed the skull in their collection was an ancient treasure. But now they think it's a modern fake.

© RIK HAMILTON / ALAMY

Washington, DC, USA: The skull on display at the Smithsonian National Museum of Natural History arrived mysteriously by post in 1992. It had an anonymous note claiming it came from Aztec times. It is the largest of the

skulls, about 38 cm high and weighing in at fourteen kilos. The museum thinks it is a fake – so much so that they even included it in an exhibition called 'Modern Fakes'

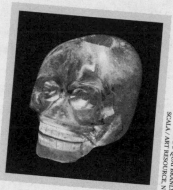

Musée du Quai Branly, Paris: The Paris skull is small – just ten cm high. But, unlike the others, it has a hole drilled through its centre, so it may have been mounted on something in the past. The museum describes it as 'Pre Columbian with Mexican origin' – so they have not declared it a fake

Skull Power

Some people believe that crystal skulls have incredible abilities. Take a look . . .

Computer Crystals

Ancient computer? No, I don't mean your very old laptop, but the skulls themselves. Some think that because the skulls are made out of the same type of quartz crystal that is inside modern-day computers, they might have a similar function. They think that their existence could even be proof of an ancient civilization even more advanced than our own.

Quartz Know-how

- More than two billion crystals are manufactured every year for use in radios, watches, clocks, mobile phones – and of course, computers – around the world
- Quartz is a vital component for a computer. Without it, computers couldn't be programmed, and memory and data could not be stored
- The quartz piece inside a computer is very small – about the size of a fingernail

So, what do you think – if a crystal chip inside a computer can store data, could a crystal skull also be a device for storing information? But how? You can't exactly plug it in . . . Some people think that we just have to discover the right way to 'read' the skulls. But at the moment, nobody knows how.

Crystal Doctor

Some believe that crystal skulls have special energies which can be used to help people, healing sickness and disease. They point to the fact that crystals were thought by ancient civilizations such as the Egyptians and the Mayans to have healing powers. Others believe that crystals have special psychic abilities and can foretell the future. But no one has ever proved any of this.

Could these ideas just be a lot of skull silliness, perhaps influenced by books – and movies like *Indiana Jones and the Kingdom of the Crystal Skull*, in which the skull of the title contains incredible knowledge and wisdom? (It also belongs to a bunch of intelligent alien archaeologists, who claim the skull back, then take off in a flying saucer – but not until they've activated a portal into another dimension and caused chaos on Earth!)

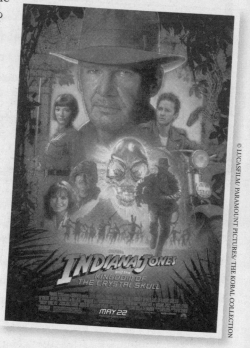

© LUCASFILM/ PARAMOUNT PICTURES/ THE KOBAL COLLECTION

It's total fiction – but are all these claims about the skulls fictional too?

MY MISSION

Let's make no bones about it (sorry) – I could do an Indiana Jones, grab myself a battered leather hat and a whip, and travel all the way to Central America to find out more about the ancient Mayans and Aztecs.

OR I could visit the British Museum in London (a handier distance from my home) to see for myself one of the legendary crystal skulls we've discussed in this book.

I think you've guessed my choice.

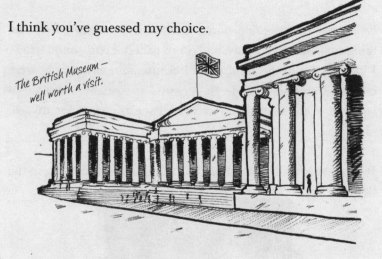

The British Museum – well worth a visit.

KIT LIST

A day trip to a museum is one of my simpler missions (phew!) so I shouldn't need too much. Just:

- 🔍 A BRITISH MUSEUM GUIDE BOOK – it's a big place so this will help me find my way around

- COMFY SHOES – lots of walking and standing involved
- BOTTLE OF WATER/SNACKS IN A BACKPACK – need to keep those energy levels up
- TRAVELCARD – to get me there and back on the London Underground
- NOTEBOOK AND PEN
- MAGNIFYING GLASS – to get an even better close-up view of the crystal skull

MISSION COMPLETED

Using my trusty guide book, I made my way to where the famous skull is on display, in a room called 'Living and Dying'. I knew I was in the right place because so many people were clustered around a single glass case. I eventually managed to squeeze in through the crowds and see the skull for myself, close up.

It was a beautiful sight, about 25 cm high, and sparkling in the light.

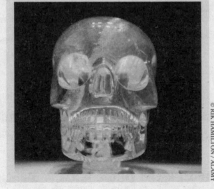

© RIK HAMILTON / ALAMY

The British Museum's crystal skull – a big attraction.

I found out more about the history of the skull. The British Museum bought it from Tiffany of New York in 1897, believing that it was a genuine Aztec relic, purchased from a Spanish officer in Mexico. The description on the skull says that it was originally thought to have been Aztec but is now believed to have made in the nineteenth century.

But the museum website is slightly different. It says of the skull's origin: *'The question remains open . . .'*

WHAT DO YOU THINK?

1. Crystal Skulls Are Fakes

In the 1990s the Smithsonian National Museum of Natural History and the British Museum decided to find out the truth about the crystal skulls in their collections. The skulls were closely examined by experts under light and scanning electron microscopes. They all thought the same thing: marks on both skulls showed that they had most likely been carved and polished using high-speed cutting and polishing tools called rotary wheels. These are modern tools, which weren't around

in Aztec or Mayan times. The museums decided that the skulls must have been made much later, probably in the nineteenth century.

The Mitchell-Hedges skull was examined by an expert from the Smithsonian, who also found similar 'modern' markings.

The British Museum now believes that all the crystal skulls in existence are probably fakes.

But why would someone bother to 'fake' a crystal skull?

In the nineteenth century, people became very interested in ancient cultures and their histories. Museums, collectors and shops around the world were looking to buy all kinds of interesting objects, from ancient Egyptian relics to Aztec pottery. A crystal skull would have been worth a lot of money – particularly if it was thought to come from one of the Mesoamerican civilizations.

In the late 1900s a French dealer called Eugène Boban sold some of these skulls to museums, claiming they were ancient relics, but no one knows where he got them from.

Some think they could have been made in Germany – in a town called Idar-Oberstein, to be exact, once known as the capital of the gemstone industry. In the 1870s craftsmen working here bought large numbers of quartz crystals from Brazil. Could these have been the beginnings of our crystal skulls?

But what about the skulls' mystical powers? We've heard lots of stories from people who believe in their strange abilities, but no one has put the skulls through a proper scientific test to prove it. In real life, crystal skulls do look very mysterious and it's easy to see why many believe that they are magical, supernatural objects. But I certainly didn't see any evidence of powerful energy beaming out from the British Museum skull . . . maybe it's just me?

A lot of people would really like to think that the crystal skulls are supernatural objects used centuries ago by Mayan or Aztec priests. It's just much more exciting than finding out the skulls were made about 50 years ago in a German factory! But perhaps that's all the skulls really are?

2. Crystal Skulls Are Genuine

How can anyone prove that the skulls were made by the ancient Aztecs or Mayans?

One of the big problems is how to date the skulls. For carbon-based things like bone, cloth, wood, animals and humans (yes, we're made of carbon too), archaeologists can use a method called carbon dating to work out how old something is. But there's no such test for quartz crystal. Because it doesn't decay or change over time, there's no scientific way to find out when it was made.

The main argument for the skulls being fakes is that the markings shown on the surface of the skulls look as if they have been made by modern instruments. But is this really the case?

We know that Mesoamerican civilizations did carve stone and minerals – archaeologists have discovered body decorations, like lip plugs, ear spools and beads. These were often carved from obsidian, a hard dark volcanic stone (not crystal). But while most experts don't believe that any such civilization would have used a rotary wheel cutter, a few say it's possible that they could have used some kind of wheel for carving.

Were the Mesoamericans more advanced than we think? Could they have used tools that weren't even supposed to exist more than a thousand years ago?

We know that skulls were important in both Aztec and Mayan cultures but, so far, no skull made from crystal has ever been found by archaeologists at one of their ruins. If one day a sparkling crystal skull is dug up at such a site, we'll finally have our evidence.

YOU DECIDE

Mystical objects – or modern fakes? Your decision . . .

But whatever you decide and note down at the back of the book, most people will agree that crystal skulls are beautiful objects which deserve to be on display in museums, however and whenever they were made.

WANT TO KNOW MORE?

Tutankhamun – The Life and Death of a Pharaoh – David Murdoch (Dorling Kindersley)

King Tut's Curse! – Jacqueline Morley (Book House)

The Life and World of Tutankhamen – Brian Williams (Heinemann)

Eyewitness Guide: Pirate – Richard Platt (Dorling Kindersley)

Fact or Fiction: Pirates – Stewart Ross (Aladdin/Watts)

Terror on the Amazon – The Quest for El Dorado – Phil Gates (DK Readers)

Sir Walter Raleigh and the Quest for El Dorado – Marc Aronson (Houghton Mifflin)

Unexplained: An Encyclopedia of Curious Phenomena, Strange Superstitions and Ancient Mysteries – Judy Allen (Kingfisher)

www.britishmuseum.org

www.nationalgeographic.com – Great for all kinds of information about the world. You can search the site for their views on the mysteries in this book.

DECISION TIME

So, we've looked at the evidence (which sometimes got a bit too close for comfort, if you ask me). Now it's time for you to sort the facts from the fiction and solve some of the world's greatest mysteries once and for all . . .

Mystery 1: Pirate Treasure

Notes:

_____

_____

Possible explanations:

☐ *1. There Is Pirate Treasure Out There Still*

☐ *2. Pirate Treasure Is a Myth*

☐ *3. Other* _____

Mystery 2: The Curse of the Pharaohs

Notes:

_____

_____

Possible explanations:

☐ *1. The Curse of Tutankhamen Doesn't Exist*

☐ *2. The Tombs Are Toxic*

☐ *3. The Curse Is Real!*

☐ *4. Other* _____

Mystery 3: The Legend of El Dorado

Notes:

_____

_____

_____

_____

_____

_____

Possible explanations:

☐ *1. El Dorado Is a Myth*

☐ *2. El Dorado Exists*

☐ *3. Other* _____

_____

Mystery 4: The Crystal Skull Conundrum

Notes:

_____

_____

_____

_____

_____

_____

_____

_____

Possible explanations:

☐   *1. Crystal Skulls Are Fakes*

☐   *2. Crystal Skulls Are Geniune*

☐   *3. Other* _____

If you enjoyed this book, why not try
the other titles in the series?

GREAT MYSTERIES OF THE WORLD

ALIEN ENCOUNTERS
CREEPY CREATURES
WEIRD WATERS

Read every out-of-this-world adventure!

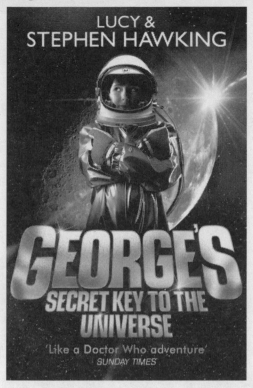

Take a ride through space and discover the mysteries of science and the universe with George and a super-intelligent computer called Cosmos.

But someone else would like to get their hands on Cosmos – someone whose power-hungry plans will lead George to a black hole and sure-fire deep space danger.

George's best friend Annie needs help.
She has discovered something really weird
on her dad's super-computer.

Is it a message from an alien? Could there be
life out there? And if you could talk to aliens,
what would you say?

**Meet Itch – an accidental, accident-prone hero.
Science is his weapon. Elements are his gadgets.**

Richard Hammond invites you to journey with him to the planet's most puzzling places . . .

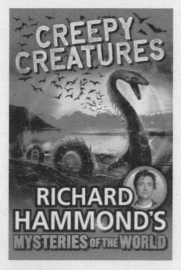

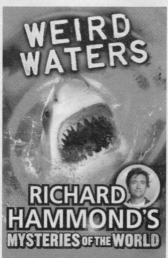

Can you solve the mystery?